AN ELLIS ISLAND TIME CAPSULE

ARTIFACTS OF THE HISTORY OF IMMIGRATION

by Rachael Hanel

Consultant:
Richard Bell, PhD
Associate Professor of History
University of Maryland, College Park

CAPSTONE PRESS

Capstone Captivate is published by Capstone Press, an imprint of Capstone.
1710 Roe Crest Drive
North Mankato, Minnesota 56003
www.capstonepub.com

Library of Congress Cataloging-in-Publication Data is available
on the Library of Congress website.
ISBN: 978-1-5435-9229-0 (library binding)
ISBN: 978-1-4966-6627-7 (paperback)
ISBN: 978-1-5435-9236-8 (eBook pdf)

Summary: The artifacts of Ellis Island tell the story of millions of immigrants who passed through its halls on their journey to a new life in the United States. Imagine discovering a time capsule filled with items including a worn cap, yellowed letters, and old dinnerware. Explore these items and more to learn about the experience of journeying through Ellis Island in the early 1900s.

Image Credits
Alamy: Contraband Collection, 30, Melissa Jooste, 6, Science History Images, 32, Tracy Carncross, 9; Getty Images: Bettmann, 43, Corbis/George Rinhart, 34, Hulton Archive, 39; Granger: 17, 18, 36; Library of Congress: 10, 23, 25, 27, 41; National Park Service: Statue of Liberty National Monument and Ellis Island, cover (top right), 14, 16, 22, 26, 37; The New York Public Library: cover (middle), 5, 28, 38; Newscom: Everett Collection, 31; Shutterstock: ale-kup (background), cover and throughout, Everett Historical, 19, 20, 21, littlenystock, 42; Smithsonian American Art Museum: Transfer from the U.S. Capitol, cover (left), 12; Smithsonian Institution: National Museum of American History/ Division of Medicine and Science, 24

Editorial Credits
Editor: Julie Gassman; Designer: Lori Bye; Media Researcher: Svetlana Zhurkin; Production Specialist: Tori Abraham

Table of Contents

CHAPTER 1

INTRODUCTION 4

CHAPTER 2

THE IMMIGRANT JOURNEY 6

CHAPTER 3

ARRIVAL 14

CHAPTER 4

PROCESSING 18

CHAPTER 5

DETENTION 30

CHAPTER 6

CONCLUSION 39

More About the Artifacts............................44
Glossary...46
Read More 47
Internet Sites...47
Index...48

Words in **bold** are in the glossary.

INTRODUCTION

When something important happens, we want to remember it. One of the ways we can do that is to save special things from that event. Artifacts such as **advertisements**, uniforms, and even toys can be pieces of evidence that help prove what happened. They can show how people reacted and remind us what was important about that moment in time. This collection of items could even be kept in a time capsule—a container of artifacts buried away for discovery in the future.

What if there were a special time capsule for each important moment in history? What if you found one of these time capsules? What might be in it?

From 1892 to 1954, Ellis Island served an important role in American history. This small piece of land in New York **Harbor** was the first stop for millions of **immigrants**. Ellis Island served as a gate that immigrants had to go through before entering the United States.

At Ellis Island, **inspectors** checked and questioned every single immigrant. If they passed inspection, they were allowed into the United States. If immigrants didn't pass, they were sent back home. If there was a time capsule to help you understand the immigrant journey, what might be in it?

From the Time Capsule:
LETTER FROM
AN IMMIGRANT

TIME CAPSULE
ARTIFACT:
IMMIGRANT LETTER

The first item you might pull out could be a letter. It was written by a recent immigrant to the United States to a relative back in Finland. Letters were the only way to maintain connections between relatives. The letters from the United States often mentioned the many jobs available and the beautiful scenery. This often encouraged relatives back home to come to the United States themselves.

Each immigrant left home for different reasons. Some wanted to escape war. Others didn't have enough food. Many had very little money. But they all had one thing in common: They had all heard of America as the land of opportunity.

The long journey started at home. First, immigrants had to decide what to take with them. They knew there would be little room on the ship. Many immigrants carried only a small bag. Then they had to say goodbye to family and friends who were staying behind. Often this would be the last time they would ever see mothers and fathers, grandmothers and grandfathers.

Next, many immigrants had to travel by train or **carriage** for hours or days to a harbor city. There, they would board a ship and sail to the United States.

FACT

Ellis Island Immigration Station opened on January 1, 1892. The first immigrant to be processed was 15-year-old Annie Moore, who was from County Cork, Ireland.

The next item in the time capsule might be a colorful poster. It advertises an ocean liner that took people to the United States. An illustration of the ship takes up almost the entire poster.

TIME CAPSULE
ARTIFACT:
POSTER

Crowded ocean liners held as many as 3,000 passengers, most of them immigrants, on each journey across the Atlantic Ocean.

You might have a hard time imagining just how big these ships were. What a sight that must have been! Traveling across the ocean was a once-in-a-lifetime experience for immigrants.

Most immigrants could afford only the least expensive tickets. The cheapest tickets were in third class (also known as steerage). An immigrant might have to save money for weeks or even months before buying a ticket.

Life on the ship was not as pretty as imagined from the poster. Hundreds of people huddled together for the one- to two-week journey across the ocean. Passengers in third class slept on bunk beds crammed into big rooms. Mattresses were just thin coverings of fabric over straw or seaweed. Food was served on **deck** from large pails. Many people became seasick. Violent storms frightened passengers. But they knew they were almost "home" when a wonderful sight came into view: the Statue of Liberty.

From the Time Capsule:
SMALL VERSION OF THE STATUE OF LIBERTY

From the time capsule, you might pull out a sculpture that looks like a smaller version of the Statue of Liberty. The larger sculpture greeted immigrants as they approached the harbor. You can imagine what it was like for immigrants to see the grand sight. Passengers on the ships cheered when the 305-foot- (93-meter-) tall statue first came into view.

TIME CAPSULE ARTIFACT:
STATUE

That meant they had made it to America. The Statue of Liberty is located on Liberty Island, right next to Ellis Island. The copper statue was completed in July 1884 and arrived in New York Harbor in June 1885. It was a gift from France.

A poem at the base of the statue has welcomed immigrants since 1903. The poem, titled "The New Colossus," was written by Emma Lazarus. Part of it reads:

Give me your tired, your poor,
Your huddled masses yearning to breathe free,
The wretched refuse of your teeming shore.
Send these, the homeless, tempest-tost to me,
I lift my lamp beside the golden door!

At long last, the immigrants had arrived at America's shore. But the trek through Ellis Island was just beginning.

From the Time Capsule:
INSPECTOR'S CAP

As you reach into the time capsule, your fingers could feel something scratchy, like wool. You feel around a bit more and realize it's a cap. When you examine it, it almost looks like it could be part of a military uniform. There's a **crest** sewn on the front, with the word *INSPECTOR* underneath it. The initials above the crest, *U.S.I.S.*, stand for "United States Immigration Service." The person who wore this cap was an **inspector** who boarded the ship once it docked in the harbor.

TIME CAPSULE
ARTIFACT:
INSPECTOR'S CAP

Passengers couldn't leave the ship until inspectors came on board. One inspector quickly scanned the crowd, looking for any signs of illness. Another inspector was in charge of **customs**. This was to make sure the ship's **cargo** did not contain illegal goods that shouldn't be brought into the country.

Another set of inspectors and doctors came on board to check the passengers from first and second class. These passengers paid more money for their tickets. They had better places to sleep and better food to eat than the third-class passengers. They also were inspected on the ship and didn't have to go to Ellis Island. But the passengers in third class had many hours in front of them, perhaps even days, before they could finally enter the United States.

After you lay the cap aside, you might reach in the time capsule and feel something soft. In your hands you hold a cuddly teddy bear. Immigrant children often brought a treasured toy from home. The toys were something familiar to have in this strange, new place.

TIME CAPSULE
ARTIFACT:
TEDDY BEAR

The journey was especially difficult for children traveling in steerage. Though they could play together, they were often tired and hungry.

It was a special treat to be able to bring a toy because there was little room for anything extra in the luggage. A child might have only a small bag. Adults might have bigger bags, or maybe even a trunk. Adults often brought household goods, such as dishes, pots, and candlesticks. They also liked to bring family **heirlooms**, such as a lace tablecloth or a prayer book. People often tucked family photos into their bags.

From the Time Capsule:
LANDING CARD

Once passengers were inspected, it was time to leave the ship. Perhaps you look into the time capsule and see a thin piece of paper. It is just a few inches long and has a number printed on it. A safety pin sticks out at the top. This tag was pinned to each immigrant's clothing while they were still on the ship. The number matched the person's name according to the ship's manifest, or passenger list. This tag remained on each person throughout the inspection process on Ellis Island.

Red Star Line

Landing Card

MAJESTIC
Manifest Sheet No.

C 22

Name
Levenfish Mirriam

List Number   2

TIME CAPSULE
ARTIFACT:
LANDING CARD

Having a landing card cleared an immigrant to enter Ellis Island and continue the inspection process.

FACT

The busiest day at Ellis Island was April 17, 1907. Exactly 11,747 immigrants were processed that day. That year was also the peak year, with just over 1 million immigrants processed.

Immigrants often had to wait several hours or even days for a spot on a ferry to Ellis Island.

Immigrants were taken from the big ships by **ferries** to Ellis Island. The ferry was like a "floating waiting room." If immigrants were lucky, they arrived at the island and could quickly leave the ferry. But if the lines for processing were long, immigrants might have to wait on the ferry for hours until there was room for them. The ferries did not have roofs. Immigrants waited in all weather conditions, from the extreme heat of summer to the brutal cold of winter.

Angel Island Immigration Station

Not all immigrants came to the United States through New York City. For immigrants coming from Asia, it made sense to come through California. The Angel Island Immigration Station was located just outside of San Francisco. It was open from 1910 to 1940 and served an estimated 340,000 immigrants, most of them from China. The island is now a state park.

As at Ellis Island, passengers were inspected on the ships before entry to Angel Island.

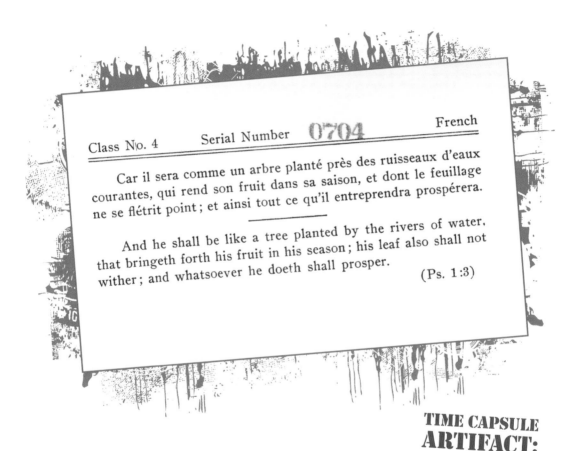

Class No. 4   Serial Number   0704   French

Car il sera comme un arbre planté près des ruisseaux d'eaux courantes, qui rend son fruit dans sa saison, et dont le feuillage ne se flétrit point ; et ainsi tout ce qu'il entreprendra prospérera.

And he shall be like a tree planted by the rivers of water, that bringeth forth his fruit in his season; his leaf also shall not wither; and whatsoever he doeth shall prosper.

(Ps. 1:3)

TIME CAPSULE
ARTIFACT:
LITERACY TEST CARD

The next thing you might see in the time capsule is a piece of paper. It is the size of an index card with words printed on it. At the top are words in a different language. Underneath that text you see English words.

The card is a literacy test. Starting in 1917, immigrants older than 16 had to prove they could read. Members of Congress passed a law because they only wanted immigrants who had some education. They were trying to keep out as many immigrants as possible. People who opposed the law thought it didn't make sense. Even if people couldn't read, they still could work. Very few people failed the test anyway.

By 1917, more people around the world than ever before had access to school and education. That made it likely they could read once they came to the United States.

A 1916 political cartoon was critical of the literacy test.

The next item you might remove from the time capsule is a stethoscope. Each immigrant had to be examined for signs of illness. If someone was sick, they couldn't enter the United States.

TIME CAPSULE
ARTIFACT:
STETHOSCOPE

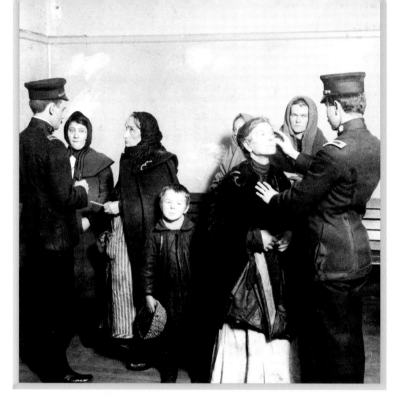
Women and children were examined separately from men.

The medical inspection process was fast. For example, doctors with stethoscopes listened to a person's heart. If the heartbeat didn't sound normal, the person's clothing was marked with an *H* with a piece of chalk. If a person had an eye disease, the doctor would mark the person's clothing with an *E*.

Immigrants were afraid to be marked with the chalk. If they were, they had to go into another line for a more complete medical inspection. This would delay their entry into the United States. It also meant they were separated from their families.

TIME CAPSULE
ARTIFACT:
INSPECTOR'S DESK

Immigrants who passed literacy tests and medical inspection then went to the final step: one last inspection. In the time capsule you might find a tall wooden desk. An inspector stood behind this desk and asked immigrants a series of questions.

The stop at an inspector's desk was the final step in the immigration process at Ellis Island.

These questions included "What is your name?" and "What do you plan to do in the United States?" For immigrants who didn't speak English, interpreters **translated** the questions into different languages.

FACT

It's a myth that Ellis Island inspectors changed immigrants' names to make them more "American." Names actually weren't recorded at Ellis Island.

After passing inspection, immigrants had to wait once again—this time for transportation off the island.

Once the inspector gave immigrants final approval, they were free to enter the United States. For the majority of immigrants, the entire process from getting off the ferry to the final inspection lasted three to five hours. Immigrants had many options once they left Ellis Island.

About two-thirds of immigrants chose to settle outside of New York City. Many of them headed to the Midwest or the Northeast. Some had family members waiting for them in those places. Others hoped to find a job.

Twelve railroad companies operated from a ticket office on the island. Once immigrants had their tickets, they rode on a ferry across the harbor to the railroad station. They were free to pursue a new life. But not everyone was that lucky.

FACT

Immigrants were put on a three-year probation period after arrival. If they came upon hard times and couldn't work, they could be sent back to their home country. They could also be sent back if they were convicted of a crime while in the United States.

CHAPTER 5

DETENTION

From the Time Capsule:
INSPECTION CARD

Some immigrants were forced to stay on Ellis Island for days, weeks, and sometimes even months. Perhaps you pull out a small, wrinkled card next. It is labeled "inspection card" and across it you see a red stamp that says "sent to hospital."

TIME CAPSULE
ARTIFACT:
INSPECTION CARD

INSPECTION CARD
(Immigrants and Steerage Passengers).

The East-Asiatic Company, Limited.
BALTIC AMERICA LINE.

Port of departure, DANZIG. S. S. Estonia
Name of ship,
Name of Immigrant,
Date of departure,
Last residence,

Inspected and passed ad
DANZIG.
UNITED STATES
Seal Stamp by PUBLIC SERVICE
Medical Officer

Passed at quarantine, port of

SENT TO HOSPITAL
DEC 4 1925

Passed by Immigration Bureau
port of

(The following to be filled in by ship's surgeon or agent prior to or after embarcation).

Ship's list or manifest   No. on ship's list or manifest

Berth No.

About 10 percent of immigrants were sent to the hospital for further medical inspection.

If immigrants were ill, they had to stay in the Ellis Island hospital. They weren't allowed into the country until they got better. By 1911, the hospital had 275 beds. Another hospital opened that year for immigrants who had **contagious** diseases such as measles or scarlet fever.

FACT

From 1900 to 1954, 3,500 people died on Ellis Island. Of those, 1,400 were children. But 355 babies were born there too.

Hospital buildings at Ellis Island housed medical labs.

The hospitals on Ellis Island were just as good as hospitals in the mainland United States. Trained doctors and nurses worked there. The hospitals had X-ray machines and operating rooms. Thousands of patients were admitted each year.

Immigrants were kept on the island for other reasons. If a child was admitted to the hospital, one or both parents had to stay on the island. They slept on bunk beds with hundreds of other people in the same big room. Immigrants who didn't have enough money had to stay until they could get a certain amount of money. Aid societies with offices on the island helped people who didn't have enough money. Single women were not allowed to leave until a relative came to pick them up.

FACT

The first female doctor to work on Ellis Island was Dr. Rose Bebb. She began work there in 1914. She was one of the first female doctors employed anywhere in the United States.

TIME CAPSULE
ARTIFACT:
CLASSROOM PHOTO

Perhaps the next time you peer into the time capsule, you notice a photograph. You take it out and look carefully at the scene. There's a long hallway with high, stone walls and two American flags at the far end. Children sit in chairs that line the walls. You see a chalkboard and a woman sitting next to one of the children. This is a scene of a temporary classroom, and it doesn't look like any classroom you've seen.

Children who had to wait on Ellis Island for weeks, or even months, while a parent was in an island hospital had the option of attending school. School was used to keep the children busy.

Singing American songs helped children pass the time while separated from their parents.

Many of the children didn't speak or read English, so they were taught the language. The children also did arts and crafts, sang songs, and learned about American heroes. Children often were told that the United States was a great country. It was never too early to make these future citizens proud to be Americans.

The last thing you might take out of the time capsule is similar to something you probably use every day. It's a dinner plate, but this one was used daily on Ellis Island. The heavy, white plate looks fancy, and the immigration station is painted on it.

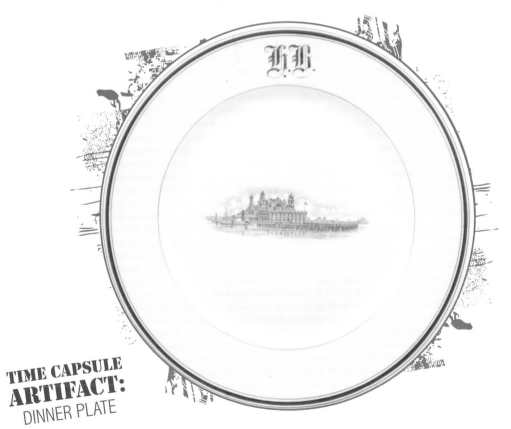

TIME CAPSULE ARTIFACT: DINNER PLATE

The hundreds of people staying on the island needed to eat. The dining room at Ellis Island could seat 1,200 people at one time. Long tables with benches filled the room. Meals were simple and hearty. Each day people would be served vegetables, some type of meat, such as bologna or lamb, and tea or coffee. For many immigrants, this was their first taste of the food they would come to eat in the United States. New foods included ice cream and white bread.

The meals the immigrants were served were free of charge.

CHAPTER 6
CONCLUSION

Ellis Island was used less and less by the early 1950s. Its daily population fell to only about 250 people. It cost too much money to keep the buildings open for so few people, so the federal government shut down Ellis Island in 1954. After that, the buildings were abandoned. Wind and rain damaged the structures. Walls started to crumble. Garbage and trash washed up on the island.

When Ellis Island was shut down in 1954, hallways were left filled with discarded equipment and flaking paint.

Peak Years of Immigration

Though Ellis Island was open from 1892 to 1954, the number of immigrants coming through started to decline dramatically in 1924. That was the year Congress passed the National Origins Act. This act put a limit on the number of immigrants who could come to the United States. It also allowed potential immigrants to be screened and processed in their home countries before coming to the United States. From 1924 to 1954, Ellis Island was used mostly as a detention center for immigrants who didn't have proper paperwork. It also held "**enemies of the state**" during World War II (1939–1945).

FACT

Ellis Island employed hundreds of workers. People were needed to inspect immigrants, feed them, and keep the grounds and buildings clean.

Lyndon B. Johnson

President Lyndon B. Johnson named Ellis Island a national monument in 1965. Plans were made in the early 1980s to fix the buildings in time for the 100th anniversary of the Statue of Liberty in 1986. The Ellis Island National Museum of Immigration opened in 1990. Visitors from around the world can go to the museum to learn more about Ellis Island and immigration history.

The large windows and tiled ceiling give Ellis Island's Registry Room a look of grandeur today. But for immigrants, the room was loud and crowded as thousands of people filed through it each day.

FACT

Ellis Island is now 27.5 acres (11.1 hectares). The number of buildings grew from one in 1892 to 41 by the time it closed in 1954.

After passing inspection at Ellis Island in 1925, a family looks toward New York City, ready to begin their new life in the United States.

For many years, Ellis Island served as the first stop for immigrants on their way to the United States. For some of them, it was an island of tears. This was because they had to stay in the hospital and were separated from their families. About two percent of all immigrants who came to Ellis Island were sent back home because they didn't have any money or had a disease doctors couldn't treat.

But for the vast majority of immigrants, Ellis Island was an island of hope. Everyone who came through Ellis Island was looking for a better life in the United States.

More About the Artifacts

Letter from an Immigrant

This letter was written by Sven Lonnberg to Paavo Lonnberg in 1899. It is an example of letters written to relatives back home. It is located in the Ellis Island National Museum of Immigration.

Poster Advertisement

This poster advertises tickets for a ship named the SS *Statendam*, one of many ships in the Holland-America Line. The shipping company was founded in 1873. The SS *Statendam* was launched in 1898. This poster is located in the Ellis Island museum.

Small Version of the Statue of Liberty

Sculptor Frédéric-Auguste Bartholdi brought this small version of his famous statue to Washington, D.C., in 1884, where it was on display in the U.S. Capitol until 1887. It measures 46 by 12 by 11 inches (117 x 30 x 28 centimeters) and is made of painted terra-cotta and tin. Today it is in the Smithsonian American Art Museum collection in Washington, D.C.

Inspector's Cap

This navy-colored cap was worn by an inspector on Ellis Island. It is on display at the Ellis Island National Monument gallery.

Teddy Bear

This teddy bear was a treasured toy brought to the United States by 9-year-old Gertrude Schneider, who emigrated with her family from Switzerland. She donated the teddy bear to the Ellis Island museum in 1988, saying, "I loved that teddy bear more than anything else."

Landing Card

This landing card was issued to immigrant Miriam Levenfish in 1923. Levenfish sailed to the United States on a Red Star Line ship. The back of the card features instructions to display it in several languages.

Literacy Test

This literacy test card contains a verse from the Book of Psalms in the Bible. At the top, the verse is written in French. The card dates from around 1917, when literacy tests were first given at Ellis Island.

Stethoscope

This stethoscope dates from around 1900 and is the type used in Ellis Island health inspections. It is made of metal, rubber, and some fabric. This artifact can be found at the National Museum of American History in Washington, D.C.

Inspector's Desk

Inspector's desks were made out of wood, and inspectors stood behind them. This desk is located at the Ellis Island museum.

Inspection Card

This inspection card was issued in 1925 to a passenger on the *Estonia*, a ship from the Baltic-America Line. The passenger, originally from Poland was sent to an Ellis Island hospital directly from the ship because of an illness.

Photo of a Temporary Classroom

This photograph was taken sometime around 1920. There were not actual classrooms on Ellis Island, so the children sat at desks wherever there was some room. In this case, they are sitting in a hallway.

Dinner Plate

This is an example of a dinner plate used at Ellis Island. Immigrants who had to stay on the island for days, weeks, or even months were fed in the dining hall. This plate is located at the Ellis Island museum.

Glossary

advertisement (ad-vuhr-TYZ-muhnt)—a published notice that gives information about goods or services

cargo (KAHR-go)—items on a ship that are transported from one place to another

carriage (KAYR-ij)—a vehicle pulled by horses

contagious (kun-TAY-juss)—spreadable, as in disease

crest (KREST)—a symbol that suggests importance

customs (KUHS-tuhms)—a restriction on items that can come into a country

deck (DEK)—the upper part of a ship

enemy of the state (EN-uh-mee UHV THUH STAYT)—a person accused of certain crimes against a government

ferry (FAYR-ee)—boat that can move in shallow water

harbor (HAR-bur)—a place where ships load and unload passengers and cargo

heirloom (AIR-loom)—item handed down from one generation to another

immigrant (IM-uh-gruhnt)—someone who comes from one country to live permanently in another

inspector (in-SPEK-tur)—someone who checks or searches things or people

translate (TRANS-late)—to change one language into a different one

Read More

Burgan, Michael. *Ellis Island: An Interactive History Adventure*. North Mankato, MN: Capstone, 2013.

Demuth, Patricia Brennan. *What Was Ellis Island?* New York: Penguin Workshop, 2014.

Kravitz, Danny. *In the Shadow of Lady Liberty: Immigrant Stories from Ellis Island*. North Mankato, MN: Capstone, 2016.

Nau, Myrna. *Questions and Answers About Ellis Island*. New York: PowerKids Press, 2018.

Internet Sites

Interactive Tour of Ellis Island
http://teacher.scholastic.com/activities/immigration/tour/

National Park Service: Ellis Island
https://www.nps.gov/elis/learn/historyculture/index.htm

U.S. History: Ellis Island
https://www.ducksters.com/history/us_1800s/ellis_island.php

Index

Angel Island Immigration Station, 21

Bartholdi, Frédéric-Auguste, 44
Bebb, Rose, 33
births, 31
buildings, 39, 40, 41, 42

chalk marks, 25
children, 16–17, 31, 33, 35–36, 45
contagious diseases, 31
customs, 15

deaths, 31
dining hall, 38, 45
dinner plate, 37, 45
doctors, 15, 25, 32, 33

education, 23, 35–36, 45
Ellis Island National Museum of Immigration, 41, 44, 45
enemies of the state, 40

families, 7, 8, 25, 28, 33, 43, 44
ferries, 20, 29
first-class passengers, 15
food, 7, 11, 15, 37–38, 45

heirlooms, 17
hospitals, 30–33, 35, 43, 45

illnesses, 15, 24–25, 30–33, 45
inspection cards, 30, 45
inspections, 5, 15, 18, 24–25, 26–28, 40, 45
inspectors, 5, 14–15, 27, 28, 40, 44, 45
interpreters, 27

jobs, 7, 23, 28, 29, 40
Johnson, Lyndon B., 41

landing cards, 18, 44
languages, 22, 27, 36, 44, 45
Lazarus, Emma, 13
letters, 7, 44

Levenfish, Miriam, 44
literacy tests, 22–23, 45
Lonnberg, Paavo, 44
Lonnberg, Sven, 44

money, 7, 11, 15, 33, 39, 43
Moore, Annie, 8

names, 18, 27
National Origins Act (1924), 40
"The New Colossus" poem, 13

peak years, 19, 40
personal items, 8, 16–17, 44
posters, 9, 44
probation period, 29
processing time, 20, 28

questions, 5, 26–27

relatives. *See* families.

Schneider, Gertrude, 44
second-class passengers, 15
settlement, 28–29
ships, 8, 9–11, 12, 14–15, 18, 44, 45
Statue of Liberty, 11, 12–13, 41, 44
stethoscopes, 24–25, 45

teddy bear, 16, 44
third-class passengers, 11, 15
toys, 16–17, 44
travel, 8, 9–11, 28–29, 44

workers, 32, 33, 40